Julia Starr Keddle and Martyn Hobbs

Inside Out

Video
Teacher's Book

Pre-intermediate

1/

Macmillan Education
Between Towns Road, Oxford OX4 3PP
A division of Macmillan Publishers Limited
Companies and representatives throughout the world

ISBN 0-333-95932-9

Text © Macmillan Publishers Limited 2005
Design and illustration © Macmillan Publishers Limited 2005

First published 2005

Page layout by Sarah Nicholson
Illustrated by Pete Smith/Specs Art p8 (cricket pitch);
Bill Piggins p14 (children)
Cover design by Andrew Oliver

The author and publishers would like to thank the following
for permission to reproduce their photographs: Steve Davies;
Damien D'Oliveria; Alamy p20 (br); Corbis p20 (tl, bl); Getty
p20 (tr).

Printed and bound in Great Britain by Martins the Printers Ltd,
Berwick upon Tweed
2009   2008   2007   2006   2005
10 9 8 7 6 5 4 3 2 1

Introduction

Welcome to the *Inside Out* Pre-intermediate Video Teacher's Book. Each level of the *Inside Out* course has its own Video and Video Teacher's Book to be used in conjunction with the *Inside Out* Student's Book. *Inside Out* videos follow the topics and content of the Student's Book and are intended to both recycle and expand language and topics from the course. There are eight video units in this book. They are related to units 1, 4, 7, 9, 12, 14, 17 and 18 of the Student's Book. For ease of reference, the unit numbers have been kept the same in the Video Teacher's Book.

The aims of the *Inside Out* videos are:

- to provide students with a stimulating and engaging learning tool that adds extra interest and variety to lessons.

- to expose students to authentic English, carefully matched to their language ability – the video units are a language-rich resource for students to extract real words and phrases from.

- to provide information on cultural aspects of language, both directly through culture-focused activities and indirectly through inferring from the video for discussion and cross-cultural comparison.

- to give students a more in-depth knowledge of the topics and texts in the Student's Book thereby enabling them to make a fuller, better-informed contribution in class.

- to offer students the chance to increase their confidence by watching and understanding native speakers in context.

Inside Out Videos

The *Inside Out* videos are closely linked to the topics and activities in the Student's Book. Each video unit lasts approximately five minutes, but may vary from unit to unit. In order to help you find the unit you want to use, the running time is indicated in the bottom left-hand corner of the screen and the unit number can be found in the top left-hand corner.

Each video unit stands alone as a complete lesson, and together with the worksheet activities should take between 30 and 45 minutes. The videos contain a variety of genres such as documentaries, interviews and dramas, and include monologues, conversations and narratives. They can be divided into four categories: 'extension' units, 'specialised subject' units, 'drama' units and 'anecdote' units.

- Extension units develop and extend topics or reading texts in the Student's Book. For example, in Student's Book unit 1, the first two pages are all about names. Video unit 1 has six people talking about the origin and meaning of their names.

- Specialised subject units pick up one thread of a topic that a Student Book unit is based on. For example, Student's Book unit 4 is all about sport with some articles about fitness and a reading text about golf. Video unit 4 is all about one sport, cricket, and how players keep fit and learn to play the game.

- Drama units dramatise the subject in the Student's Book. For example, in Student's Book unit 7, there is a reading text about nightmare jobs. Video unit 7 is a mini-drama about a worker who returns to work after a holiday and has a disastrous day.

- Anecdote units show anecdotes from the Student's Book being performed by native speakers. They can be used to provide a model or for comparison. For example, in Student's Book unit 12, the anecdote is all about confessions. Video unit 12 has five people making confessions about things they did when they were younger.

Inside Out Video Teacher's Book

The Video Teacher's Book contains everything you need to fully exploit the video. The photocopiable worksheets include:

- a variety of activities that guide students through the unit and develop their understanding of the topics and language in the video. There are two pages of activities per unit.

- Before You Watch activities that lead students into the video via discussion or prediction or by pre-teaching vocabulary essential to understanding the video.

- While You Watch activities that exploit the video through a clearly sequenced variety of activity types. Students are usually asked to watch the video twice. On the first viewing students are frequently given a global watching task that enables them to focus on the video rather than on the worksheet. For example: ticking pictures shown in the video, ordering pictures or events and matching names and pictures. This is to help students gain a general understanding of the content while providing a video-focused task to engage students' attention. On the second viewing, students are given tasks that require them to watch for detail in order to deepen their understanding of the video. If students have difficulty with any of these watching-for-detail activities, you may want to play that particular section again.

Where the video exploitation is divided into parts, the times are shown on the worksheet.

- After You Watch activities that are directly related to the video and ask students to give their personal reaction to it by comparing what they have seen with their own situation, personalising the topic or generalising from the video. This stage of the worksheet may also include work on lexis from the video.

The teacher's notes include:

- a summary of the video content and guidance on how to use the video in conjunction with the Student's Book. The videos can be used at different points in the Student's Book and there are clear suggestions in the teacher's notes on when to use them.

- a language focus section giving a list of new lexis or lexical areas (usually no more than twelve words or phrases), and where appropriate the language area highlighted by the video. No new grammar items are introduced in the videos or worksheets.

- background cultural information on the video that the teacher may use to introduce the video or to answer any questions students may have about a particular cultural aspect contained in the video. These may be used at a suitable point during the video activities or at the end of the class to test students' observation and understanding.

- a full answer key.

- a tapescript of the video which may be photocopied and ...

  - given to students to read through and pick out any language they found useful or new to them.

  - used by the students to follow the video.

  - used by the teacher to create additional activities for use with the video, for example, additional gap-fill activities or comprehension questions.

General video techniques

Even though the *Inside Out* Video Teacher's Book provides teachers with a wide variety of activities, here are three more general video techniques that can be used at points you think are appropriate. For all three you will need to watch the video first and choose the best sequence to use the technique with.

Freeze frame

Pause the video at a moment of your choice. You can then ...

- ask the students to predict what happens next.

- check the students' understanding of the unit by asking them to summarise what they have seen.

- ask the students to describe the picture, focus on a vocabulary item or on a point of cultural interest.

Sound down

Use the TV mute control to view a sequence without sound. You can then ask the students ...

- to reconstruct a conversation.

- to discuss what the people are talking about.

- to decide on a soundtrack or script to accompany the pictures.

Vision off

Use the TV brightness control to darken the screen until no picture is visible, but the students can still hear the sound. You can then ask the students ...

- to say what they think is happening in the sequence.

- to make a storyboard (a series of drawings) showing how they would direct the sequence and, after watching the sequence, to compare their ideas with what they saw.

Contents

Note: For ease of reference, the unit numbers above refer to the corresponding units in the *Inside Out* Student's Book.

1 Names

Before you watch

1 Divide the names into male and female.

~~Jack~~ Harald Emily James William Harry Joseph Sarah Adam Rachel Adriana Ryan Madeline Matthew Darina Alice Esme Kieran Anna Laura Charles David Claudia Katalin Rosemary

Jack

2 Work with a partner. Look at the names and answer these questions.

a) Which names do you like best?

b) Which ones don't you like at all?

While you watch

3 You are going to watch some people talking about their names. Watch and complete the information.

About my name

Matthew Davidson

Mathew's last name means 'a) _____ of David'. His first name is an Old Testament Bible name. It means 'b) _____ of God'.

Darina Richter

Darina's first name comes from Slovakia. Her c) _____ chose it. Her second name is d) _____ and means 'judge'.

Claudia Mba

Claudia's last name is her e) _____ name, and it's from f) _____ . It's got a long meaning, 'You can say what you like about leopards, but if you're faced with one then you'll still run away.' Claudia is an ancient Roman name. Her father chose it because he g) _____ Latin and Greek.

Harald Dahle

Harald's names come from h) _____ . His i) _____ name means 'the man who leads the army' and his j) _____ means 'valley'.

Katalin Süle

Katalin is a Hungarian name. Her second name is from Hungary and k) _____ . Her sister chose her first name. Her parents put different names in a l) _____ and her sister pulled out her name!

Joseph Wilson

Joseph knows the meaning of his first name – but not in m) _____ ! His last name means 'the n) _____ of Will'. His parents chose his name because they liked it.

4 Watch the video again and write the names.

a) _____'s favourite name for a girl is Esme.

b) _____'s favourite name is his wife's name.

c) _____'s favourite name is Matthew.

d) _____ wanted a different name when he was younger.

e) _____'s favourite girl's name is Madeline.

f) _____'s favourite name is Anna.

After you watch

5 Work with a partner and talk about the people in the video. What do you find surprising or interesting?

6 Work in groups and discuss these questions.

a) What's your full name?

b) Where does your name come from?

c) Does your first name mean anything?

d) Does your last name mean anything?

e) Would you like a different name?

Photocopiable

4 A new star

Before you watch

1 Read the text. Then label the diagram with the words in the box.

> 1) ~~umpire~~   2) batsman   3) bowler   4) fielder   5) wicket keeper   6) bat   7) pitch   8) wicket

Cricket is an eleven-a-side game played with a wooden bat and a hard ball. The traditional clothes are white, although professional teams now often wear colours. The main cricket countries of England, Australia, South Africa, the West Indies, New Zealand, India, Pakistan, Sri Lanka and Zimbabwe have regular matches.

Cricketers play on a large oval grass field with a 20 metre long pitch in the middle. The pitch has a 'wicket' at each end. The teams are either 'fielding' or 'batting'. The batting team tries to hit the ball to score 'runs'. Only two batsmen are on the pitch at any one time. These batsmen run between the wickets after they hit the ball and their 'runs' are counted.

The bowler bowls (throws) the ball to the batsman. A 'wicket keeper' stands behind the wicket and tries to catch the ball. Other players from the fielding team are in the field (fielders) and try to catch the ball the batsman hits. If they catch the ball, the batsman is 'out', and the next batsman plays. An umpire makes sure everyone follows the rules.

While you watch

PART 1 (06:38:00–09:00:00)

2 Watch Part 1 with the sound off and tick (✓) the items below as you see them.

- [ ] an umpire
- [ ] a bowler
- [ ] a cricket pitch
- [ ] a wicket
- [ ] a cricket ball
- [ ] a cricket bat
- [ ] a run
- [ ] a wicket keeper
- [ ] a batsman
- [ ] a fielder

3 Watch Part 1 again and answer the questions.

a) When did cricket start?
   1. the thirteenth century [ ]
   2. the fifteenth century [ ]
   3. the seventeenth century [ ]

b) When did modern cricket start?
   1. the 1900s [ ]
   2. the 1800s [ ]
   3. the 1700s [ ]

c) When was the Worcester County Cricket Club founded?
   1. 1898 [ ]
   2. 1865 [ ]
   3. 1856 [ ]

d) How long can games go on for?
   1. three hours [ ]
   2. an hour [ ]
   3. several days [ ]

Part 2 (09:00:00–10:30:00)

4 Watch Part 2, an interview with Steve Davis from the Worcester Academy team, and (circle) the correct options.

a) Steve Davis started playing cricket when he was *six / ten*.

b) He has been playing cricket for *six / twelve* years.

c) His ambition is to play for *Australia / England*.

d) Every Friday he receives a *weekly / daily* programme.

e) He usually plays *one / four* games of cricket a week.

f) He trains *every day / most days*.

g) Today Steve is *giving out / collecting* a prize.

5 Watch Part 2 again and complete Steve's answer to the question with the words in the box.

What do you love about cricket?

hard   everything   fitness   physical

'I love a) _____ about cricket. I love the b) _____ side of it. I love coming training,

working really c) _____ . I love the d) _____ side of it. I just love it all.'

Part 3 (10:30:00–11:53:00)

6 Watch Part 3, an interview with Damien D'Oliveira, the director and assistant coach of the team. Put the sentences in the order you hear them.

a) I was originally taken on by Worcester as a professional player and I played as a professional cricketer from 1982 to 1996. ☐

b) What are Steve's best points as a player? ☐

c) The fitness of the players nowadays is probably a hundred percent more than it used to be. ☐

d) What's the best thing about being a coach? ☐

e) How fit do the players have to be? ☐

f) He's obviously very talented at the job he does, i.e. batting and wicket-keeping. He moves well. He's got a very good pair of hands and has got all the makings of a top-class player. ☐

g) Identifying young talent, working with them, helping them develop, watching them develop, watching them improve. ☐

h) Damien D'Oliveira is the director and assistant coach of the academy team. ☐

After you watch

7 Work with a partner. Discuss these questions about a game you both like.

a) How many players are there in a team?

b) How do you play it?

c) How fit do you have to be?

d) How do you train?

e) What qualities does a player have to have?

Photocopiable

7 A bad day

Before you watch

1 Work with a partner. Put the words in the box under the correct headings.

| office desk manager security pass sales figures screen |
| boss meeting reception keyboard receptionist e-mail |

Place	Office equipment	Document	Person	Other
office	_____	_____	_____	_____
_____	_____	_____	_____	_____
_____			_____	

2 Work with a partner. Imagine you work in an office. Put the items in the list in order from the most serious action (10) to the least serious action (1).

a) arriving late in the morning

b) not attending a meeting

c) falling asleep in a meeting

d) surfing the net

e) chatting with your colleagues

f) not following instructions correctly

g) wearing the wrong clothes

h) forgetting your security pass

i) phoning your friends

j) having a long lunch break

Have you ever done any of these things? Tell your partner.

3 You are going to watch a mini-drama about Jack's bad day. Work with a partner. Read the sentences people say in the video. Discuss what you think goes wrong on Jack's bad day.

a) 'Here's your temporary pass.' ☐

b) 'I tried to call.' ☐

c) 'Meeting?' ☐

d) 'My plane arrived terribly late.' ☐

e) 'It's half past eleven. They're not coming, are they?' ☐

f) 'Have you found that e-mail yet?' ☐

g) 'I asked for the sales figures for Australia.' ☐

h) 'What is it? On your screen?' ☐

▭ While you watch

4 Watch the video. Are the sentences in 3 said by Jack (J), Jack's boss, Nina (N) or the receptionist (R)? Write the letters in the boxes in 3.

5 Watch the video again and put the scenes in the correct order.

After you watch

6 Match the parts of the story to the photos in 5. Write the letter of each photo in the boxes.

1) Nina stopped Jack in the corridor. She was annoyed that he was late.

2) There was supposed to be a meeting at eleven o'clock with the accounts department. Nina and Jack waited for half an hour but the people didn't come.

3) Nina came to Jack's office at the end of the day. She tried to be sympathetic. But then she saw something on his screen. Oh dear, Jack!

4) Jack went to Nina's office. He didn't have the e-mail but he had the sales figures. The wrong ones!

5) It was Monday morning and Jack was late for work. He didn't have his security pass with him. The receptionist called his boss.

6) Kim came to Jack's office. Jack dropped his coffee. Oh, no!

7 Complete these sentences from the video with the words in the box.

take disturb believe yet
terribly sure

a) Sorry to _____ you.

b) I'm _____ sorry.

c) Are you _____ you invited them?

d) Have you found that e-mail _____ ?

e) Don't _____ all day.

f) I don't _____ this!

8 Work in groups. Discuss these questions.

a) Was the receptionist too hard on Jack? Why/why not?

b) Did Jack arrange a meeting with the accounts department?

c) Were the wrong sales figures Jack's or Nina's fault? Why?

d) Was the picture of Nina on Jack's screen his fault? Why/why not?

e) Do you think Nina should have behaved differently towards Jack? How?

Photocopiable

Before you watch

1 Work in groups. What do you know about your parents' schooldays? Discuss these questions.

a) What were their favourite subjects?

b) Did they have to wear a uniform?

c) Did they study different subjects to you?

d) Did they have lunch at school?

e) Did they have to do homework?

f) What kind of punishments did they have?

⊙⊙ While you watch

PART 1 (17:40:00–18:48:00)

2 Watch Part 1 and complete the family tree with the names in the box and the ages of the children.

| Tom | Connie | John | Pauline |

a) _____   Gillian   Jeff   b) _____

c) _____   Claire   Luke   d) _____

Age e) _____   Age f) _____   Age g) _____   Age h) _____

PART 2 (18:49:00–20:47:00)

3 Watch Part 2 and decide whether these statements are true or false. Tick (✓) the boxes.

	True	False
a) Gillian's favourite subject was history.	☐	☐
b) Pauline didn't like her typing and shorthand teacher.	☐	☐
c) Tom's favourite lesson is RE.	☐	☐
d) Connie's favourite lesson is art.	☐	☐
e) Connie is studying all the subjects that her aunt, Gillian, studied.	☐	☐
f) Jeff's French teacher only had one arm.	☐	☐
g) Claire doesn't have a favourite teacher.	☐	☐
h) Mr Blunsdon is Luke's music teacher.	☐	☐

PART 3 (20:48:00–22:19:00)

4 Read the text and complete the school rules using the words in the box.

| wear | stand | smoking | gum | hour's | hit | uniform | arrive | ring | walk | move | lines |

SCHOOL RULES AND PUNISHMENTS

a) You had to _____ up as soon as the teacher came into the room, and again when they left.

b) No _____ . No alcohol on the premises.
   Do not run, always _____ .

c) You had to _____ your cap from the moment you left your home in the morning until the moment you got home at night.

d) You're not allowed to chew _____ .
   You've got to obey the teachers.

e) You have to _____ on time with everything you need. And no running, pushing. No chewing gum, and you have to wear a school _____ .

f) The teacher would shout at you, maybe even _____ you. If you'd behaved really badly, you'd be sent to the Head and you'd get a ruler over the palm of your hand.

g) You were given _____ or you had the slipper, or you had the cane.

h) They'll tell you off and then they might _____ you, and then yellow sheet, then breaktime detention, lunchtime detention, then after school detention, then they might _____ home.

i) Yes, you do have to do your homework. If you don't you'll get detention. You're meant to do an _____ homework every night.

Now watch Part 3 and check your answers.

PART 4 (22:20:00–24:00:00)

5 Watch Part 4 and (circle) the correct options.

a) The parents *enjoyed / didn't enjoy* their school dinners.

b) The children eat mainly *fast / healthy* food for school dinners.

c) The parents *had to / didn't have to* wear a school uniform.

d) The children today *have to / don't have to* wear a uniform in the summer.

e) The boys today *can sometimes / mustn't* wear trainers.

f) Luke *will probably / will probably not* send his children to the same school.

After you watch

6 Work with a partner. Say what is similar and different in the parents' and children's experience of school.

For example:
The parents had more physical punishments.

7 Work in groups. Compare the schooldays of the people in the video with your own experience of school.

For example:
Tom and Claire have to wear a uniform but I didn't.
The parents all ate in the school restaurant. I always took my own sandwiches.

Photocopiable

12 Confessions

Before you watch

1 Match the words with the definitions.

a) concoction   1 a story people tell about when they behaved badly
b) nail varnish   2 a soft round fruit
c) scissors   3 a long thin piece of wood
d) plum   4 an instrument for cutting paper, fabric, etc
e) stick   5 punishment for someone who has hurt you
f) mess   6 US English for back garden
g) revenge   7 a mixture of different ingredients
h) rocks   8 a dirty or untidy state
i) back yard   9 paint for fingernails
j) confession   10 US English for stones

While you watch

2 Watch all the confessions and match the people with the illustrations.

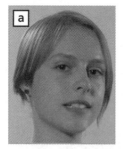    

3 Write the names.

a) Who had a sister? _____ and _____

b) Who had a friend called David? _____

c) Who lived in London? _____

d) Whose mother got very angry? _____

e) Who never told anyone about what she had done? _____

f) Who had a driver chasing him? _____

4 Watch the video again, check your answers to 3 and answer these questions.

a) Where did Darina and her friend pour all her mother's shampoos and nail varnishes?

1 in the bath

2 in the sink

3 in a bowl

b) How long was Darina kept inside as a punishment?

1 a day

2 a week

3 a month

c) Whose hair did Joanne cut?

1 her sister's

2 her sister's doll's

3 her doll's

d) How long did Joanne's sister not speak to her?

1 days

2 weeks

3 months

e) What did Joseph and his friend do with the plums?

1 play with them

2 collect them

3 eat them

f) Who told Joseph off?

1 his mother

2 the old man

3 his father

g) What did Nicola write on the wall?

1 her name

2 her sister's name

3 her doll's name

h) What did Matthew and his friends put in the snowballs?

1 small stones

2 sweets

3 nothing

After you watch

5 Work in groups. Discuss the confessions and decide which one you think is the most serious.

6 Work with a partner. Look at these phrases which were used by the people making the confessions. Tell a story from your childhood and try to use some of these phrases.

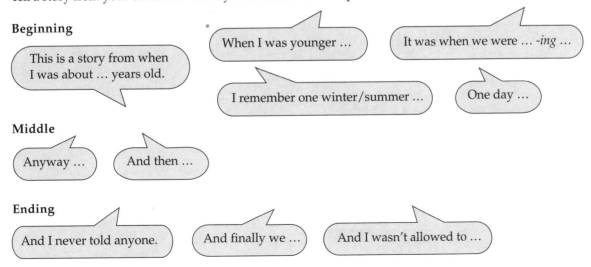

Beginning

This is a story from when I was about … years old.

When I was younger …

It was when we were … -*ing* …

I remember one winter/summer …

One day …

Middle

Anyway …

And then …

Ending

And I never told anyone.

And finally we …

And I wasn't allowed to …

Photocopiable

14　*The audition*

Before you watch

1 Think of one of your favourite films. Answer these questions.

   a) What kind of film is it? Is it action, thriller, science fiction, comedy, horror, etc?

   b) Who is the director?

   c) Who are the main actors?

   d) When does it take place – is it set in the past, present or future?

   e) What is it about?

2 Work with a partner. Tell your partner about your film.

While you watch

3 Watch the video and (circle) the correct options.

   a) The film is about *Alex King / Alex Keen*.

   b) Alex is *a film director / an actor*.

   c) Alex is trying to get a taxi to *Ealing Studios / Belsize Park*.

   d) He has *an audition / a meeting* at the studios.

   e) At the start of the film Alex feels *happy / sad* and *nervous / excited*.

   f) At the end of the film Alex feels *depressed / nervous*.

   g) Alex *does / doesn't* manage to get to the audition.

4 Work with a partner. Read the parts of the story and put them in the correct order.

   a) Alex books a cab with 1, 2, 3 Taxis to Ealing Film Studios. The woman tells him that the cab, Moscow 205, will be five minutes. ☐

   b) There aren't any taxis. Alex calls David Antonucci to say he can't get to the studios in time, but he gets David's voice mail. He leaves a message asking David to call him urgently. ☐

   c) Alex receives a call from Sarah and he tells her more about the audition. During the conversation he gets an urgent call from David Antonucci from Ealing Studios. David asks if Alex can arrive fifteen minutes earlier. Alex agrees. ☐

   d) David Antonucci calls Alex back and passes him over to Mr Spielberg. They start to speak but Alex's mobile phone battery runs out. Poor Alex! He sits on a park bench in the thunder and the pouring rain and pulls out his sandwich. Too late. No film, no stardom, no taxi. ☐

   e) Alex waits anxiously in the pouring rain for David to call back. He sees an unlocked car and he is so desperate he thinks about stealing it. He receives a good luck text message from Sarah. But this isn't his lucky day. ☐

   f) The taxi hasn't arrived yet and Alex is worried. He tries to call 1, 2, 3 Taxis but he gets a wrong number. Then he speaks to 1, 2, 3 Taxis – his cab should arrive soon. ☐

 　　Text © Macmillan Publishers Limited 2005. This sheet may be photocopied and used within the class.

g) Suddenly Alex sees his 1, 2, 3 cab arrive, but the driver doesn't stop. So Alex calls another company, Ever Ready cabs, who say a cab will take fifteen minutes. That's not quick enough to help Alex, so he doesn't book it. ☐

h) Alex King leaves a delicatessen in Belsize Park. He is on the phone to his friend Sarah. He is telling her about his exciting audition for a Steven Spielberg film. He asks her to call him back because he has to call a cab. ☐

5 Watch the video again to check your answers.

After you watch

6 Complete these phone conversations from the video with the words in the box.

> I'll   ringing   sorry   saying   It's   hear   speak   breaking   wondering   afraid

A

David: Could I a) _____ to Alex Keen, please?

Alex: King.

David: I'm sorry?

Alex: It's King. Alex King. You said Keen.

David: Oh, I'm b) _____ , Mr King. My name's David Antonucci. I'm c) _____ from Ealing Studios on behalf of Mr Spielberg.

Alex: Oh, right.

David: I was d) _____ if you could be here a quarter of an hour earlier. Mr Spielberg has another engagement and then he has to leave immediately for the airport.

Alex: No problem. e) _____ be there. I wouldn't miss this for the world.

David: Thank you very much. We'll see you soon then. Goodbye.

B

Woman: 1, 2, 3 Taxis.

Alex: Hello. f) _____ Alex King. I booked a cab over ten minutes ago.

Woman: We're doing all we can, Sir, but I'm g) _____ we're rather busy this afternoon. The cab should be with you …

Alex: Can you speak up? I can't …

Woman: … the cab should … in about …

Alex: Hold on you're h) _____ up. Hello?

Woman: Can you i) _____ me now?

Alex: Yeah, yeah, yeah.

Woman: I was just j) _____ that the cab should be with you any minute now.

Alex: You're sure? This is very urgent.

Woman: We're doing everything we can, Sir.

7 Work with a partner. Choose two of the situations and write telephone conversations. Then practise the conversations.

> dialling a wrong number

> calling a taxi

> leaving a message

> calling someone to change an appointment

Photocopiable

17 *My humans*

Before you watch

1 Work with a partner. Look at the photo of Bob, Alice and their dog Bruno. Who do you think each of the adjectives in the box applies to?

> kind   nice   intelligent   positive
> silly   loyal   independent   lazy
> fit   intellectual

While you watch

2 You are going to watch a video about a dog called Bruno. Watch the video and put the pictures in the correct order.

3 Who is Bruno talking about? Write *Bob, Alice, Candy* or *Bruno*.

a) Who gives Bruno unconditional love? _____

b) Who isn't very independent? _____

c) Who makes the important decisions? _____

d) Who is a good companion? _____

e) Who is keen on running? _____

f) Who likes asking difficult questions? _____

g) Who doesn't like tinned food? _____

h) Who doesn't like running? _____

i) Who doesn't like dogs on beds? _____

4 Tick (✓) Bruno's opinions. Then correct the ones that are wrong.

a) My humans are kind and have nice personalities. ☐

b) My humans aren't very intelligent. ☐

c) It's quite easy living with humans. ☐

d) I've always been interested in philosophical questions. ☐

e) I'm a dog of words, not actions. ☐

f) I've never been keen on convenience food. ☐

g) Your health's the most important thing. ☐

h) I prefer sleeping in my dog basket. ☐

i) I hate it when humans keep you awake during the day. ☐

5 Watch the video again and check your answers to 3 and 4.

After you watch

6 The expressions below can be used to express your opinions. Think about your daily life and complete the sentences with your own opinions. Compare your sentences with a partner.

> I like …

> I'm keen on …

> I'm not keen on …

> I worry about …

> I hate it when …

7 Complete these extracts from the video with the phrases in the box.

main problem	worry about
on the whole	unfortunately
I suppose	positive attitude

a) Alice has got a very _____ to life.

b) _____ Alice disapproves of Bruno sleeping on the bed.

c) It isn't always easy living with humans but _____ we get on very well.

d) I often _____ him because he's not very fit.

e) But the _____ is, it's not very good for you.

f) _____ I worry about it a bit because your health's the most important thing.

8 In the video we see humans from the point of view of their dog. Imagine your life from the point of view of your car/pet/computer. Choose one and write about your life.

For example:

They do really boring things with me. They take me to car parks and leave me there for hours. They always turn off the radio so I can't even listen to music …

18 Crop circles

Before you watch

1 Work in groups. Discuss these questions using the words in the box and your own ideas.

> man-made   mystery   beautiful   works of art   croppies   upset   sympathetic
> symbolic   alien communication   magnetic energy

a) How do people think landmarks like Stonehenge and crop circles are made?
b) Why have crop circles appeared?
c) Why are some people obsessed with crop circles?
d) How do farmers feel about them?
e) What do people think crop circles mean?

While you watch

2 Watch the video and put the sentences in the order you hear them.

a) Crop circles have a profound effect on people. ☐

b) The mystery and the beauty of these crop circles remains. ☐

c) Visitors are encouraged to give a donation. ☐

d) Film makers have invented special equipment. ☐

e) Crop circles can encourage you to meditate. ☐

f) Silbury Hill is the largest prehistoric earthwork in Europe. ☐

3 Answer these questions.

a) What are Silbury Hill, Avebury and Stonehenge?
1   crop circles
2   ancient monuments
3   large stones

b) When are crop circles usually created?
1   in the morning
2   in the afternoon
3   at night

c) When was the first crop circle reported?
1   1980
2   1950
3   1918

d) What kind of effect can crop circles have on people?
1   a dangerous effect
2   a calming effect
3   a serious effect

e) Why are some farmers upset by crop circles?
1   Because they lose their crops.
2   Because they get lots of visitors.
3   Because they are scared of them.

f) Which one of the following is mentioned as an explanation for crop circles.
1   They are art forms.
2   They are a part of nature.
3   They are a form of communication.

4 Work with a partner. Complete the text using some of the words in the box.

ancient   strange   magnetic   wierd
civilisations   experiences   alien

Many people believe that the aim of the circle makers is to make us all more aware of earlier a) _____ .
The crop circles are a kind of symbolic language. For them, it's no coincidence that so many crop circles are located close to b) _____ sites.

Some people think they are an
c) _____ communication.
Others believe they are created by the earth's d) _____ energies.

5 Watch the video again and check your answers to 3 and 4.

After you watch

6 Work in groups. Discuss these questions.

a) What did you think of the crop circles in the film?

b) Do they look man-made? Why/Why not?

c) What do you think of croppies (the people who study crop circles)?

d) What do you think is the best explanation for the crop circles?

Photocopiable   21

1 *Names*

Summary

This video unit could be used as support to materials in unit 1 of the Student's Book after the section *What's in a name?* It is a series of questions and answers about the names of the people interviewed.

Language focus

Questions and answers about your name:

What's your full name?

Where does your name come from?

Does your first name mean anything?

How did your parents choose your name?

Would you like a different name?

What's your favourite name?

Background information

All the people interviewed live in the UK.

Matthew is from the USA.

Darina's family is from the Czech Republic.

Claudia is from the UK but is married to someone from Nigeria.

Harald is from Norway but has lived abroad for a long time.

Katalin is from Hungary.

Joseph is from the UK.

Procedure

Before you watch

1 Ask the students to complete the table with the names.

Jack	Harald	Emily	Sarah
James	William	Rachel	Adriana
Harry	Joseph	Madeline	Darina
Adam	Ryan	Alice	Esme
Matthew	Kieran	Anna	Laura
Charles	David	Claudia	Katalin
		Rosemary	

2 Tell the students to discuss the questions. Ask some pairs to tell the rest of the class about their discussions.

While you watch

3 Ask the students to read the article and think about what the missing information might be. Then play the video and tell the students to complete the gaps.

Note: Explain that the written information is a magazine article based on the video which has people explaining their names. Ask the students to focus on the missing information, not on the exact phrasing of what the people say.

```
a) son
b) gift
c) grandmother
d) German
e) married
f) Nigeria
g) teaches
h) Norway
i) first
j) surname
k) Turkey
l) hat
m) English
n) son
```

4 Ask the students if they remember who says what. Then play the video again and tell the students to write the names.

a) Claudia	b) Harald	c) Matthew
d) Joseph	e) Darina	f) Katalin

If there is time, let the students watch the complete unit at the end so they can enjoy the whole film.

After you watch

5 Put the students into pairs to discuss the names. Examples of unusual and surprising information are the length of the meaning of Claudia's short surname; the fact that Katalin's name came from a hat and the fact that two of the English surnames originally meant 'son of'.

6 Put the students into groups and tell them to ask and answer the questions. They can take a few minutes to think about their own names and make notes before they start.

1 Names

(N = Narrator; M = Matthew; D = Darina;
C = Claudia; H = Harald; K = Katalin;
J = Joseph)

N: What's your full name?
M: Matthew J. Davidson.
N: Where does your name come from?
M: Well, I don't really know. Um, I mean obviously Davidson, son of David, um, for my last name. And Matthew is an Old Testament bible name.
N: Does your first name mean anything?
M: Yes, it does actually. It means 'gift of God'.
N: Would you like a different name?
M: No. I love my name.
N: What's your favourite name?
M: Matthew.

D: My full name is Darina Rosemary Richter. My first name comes from Slovakia. It doesn't have a special meaning, but I know my grandmother chose it. My second name is German and it means 'judge'.
N: How did your parents choose your name?
D: My grandmother chose my first name. She knew a girl that lived next door to her with the same name, and she liked it.
N: Would you like a different name?
D: No, I wouldn't.
N: What's your favourite name?
D: My favourite name is Madeline. If I have a child I think I will call her Madeline, if it's a girl.

C: My full name is Claudia Mba, which is my married name. It's a Nigerian name and it has a very long meaning even though it's a very short word. It means that you can say what you like about leopards, but if you're faced with one, then you'll still run away!
N: Does your other name mean anything?
C: No, not really. It's derived from, um, it's a Roman name and it comes from the emperor Claudius. It's a female version of that.
N: How did your parents choose your name?
C: My dad teaches Latin and Greek so I think that's probably where that one comes from.

N: Would you like a different name?
C: No, I like my name. My surname causes some problems because people never know how to pronounce it, but at least it's interesting. My favourite name for a girl is Esme, because I think it's very pretty. I don't really have a favourite boy's name.

N: What's your full name?
H: Harald Dahle.
N: And where does your name come from?
H: It comes from Norway.
N: Does your first name mean anything?
H: Um, yes, it means 'the man who leads the army'.
N: And your other names?
H: My surname means 'valley'.
N: How did your parents choose your name?
H: I don't know really.
N: Would you like a different name?
H: Not really, no.
N: What's your favourite name?
H: Adriana.
N: Why?
H: It's my wife's name.

N: What's your full name?
K: Katalin Süle.
N: Where does your name come from?
K: My first name comes from Hungary, and my second name also comes from Hungary but perhaps from Turkey too.
N: Does your first name mean anything?
K: Um, it probably does, but I don't know what it means.
N: And your other names?
K: My surname doesn't mean anything.
N: How did your parents choose your name?
K: Um, they put some names in a hat and my sister pulled my name out, my first name out.
N: Would you like a different name?
K: Um, I don't think so.
N: What's your favourite name?
K: Anna.
N: Why?
K: Um, I like the sound of it.

Inside Out

J: My full name is Joseph Vaughan Wilson.

N: Where does your first name come from?

J: I don't know.

N: Does your first name mean anything?

J: Not in English.

N: And your other name?

J: Well, I believe Wilson originally means 'son of Will' a long time ago, but now I don't think it really has any meaning.

N: How did your parents choose your name?

J: Um, I think they just chose it because it was a name they liked.

N: Would you like a different name?

J: When I was little I wanted a different name, but now I'm quite happy with it. My favourite name is probably my name, for a boy.

4 *A new star*

Summary

This video unit could be used to support material in unit 4 of the Student's Book after the *Close up*. It is a documentary about cricket and the Worcester Cricket Club. It focuses on the training of young players to be professional cricketers.

Language focus

Grammar: present simple, past simple, present perfect

Vocabulary: sport; *a coach, a player, a team, physical fitness, to train*

cricket; *batsman, bowler, fielder, pitch, umpire, wicket, wicket keeper*

Background information

The rules of cricket are very complex, but the text gives the general principles and the video provides extra information. Some other important information to know is:

- The wicket consists of three upright sticks (stumps) with two horizontal pieces of wood (bails) balanced on top.
- One run is scored when the two batsmen run from one wicket to the other.
- If they hit the ball across the boundary of the field they score four runs.
- If they hit it across the boundary without bouncing they score six runs.
- The batsman's body must not stop the ball hitting the wicket.
- If a fielder hits the wicket with the ball before the batsman reaches it, the batsman is 'out'.
- The batting team's 'innings' (batting session) is finished when 10 batsmen are 'out'.

Procedure

Before you watch

1   Put the students into pairs and brainstorm anything they know about cricket before they read the text. Ask questions such as: What colour clothes do they wear? Is it an outdoor or indoor game? Is it a ball game? Is there a bat?

Then tell the students to read the text and label the diagram using the words in the box.

> a) 5, wicket keeper   b) 2, batsman   c) 6, bat
> d) 4, fielder   e) 1, umpire   f) 8, a wicket
> g) 3, bowler   h) 7, pitch

▣ While you watch

PART 1 (06:38:00–09:00:00)

2   The aim of this exercise is to show the students in the video the things they have read about in the article. Play Part 1 with the sound off and ask the students to tick the things as they see them. Tell the class to ask for the video to be paused as they spot the things. All the items listed are visible within the first twenty seconds of the video.

3   Play Part 1 with the sound up and ask the students to answer the questions.

> a) 1
> b) 3
> c) 2
> d) 3

PART 2 (09:00:00–10:30:00)

4   Play Part 2 once before you ask the students to do the exercise. This is to familiarise them with Steve's voice and speed of delivery. Then ask them to focus on the sentences before watching the interview again.

> a) six
> b) twelve
> c) England
> d) weekly
> e) one
> f) most days
> g) giving out

5   Play Part 2 again and tell the students to complete the quote. The students may need to watch this part of the interview (10:18:00–10:30:00) several times to fill in all the gaps.

> a) everything
> b) physical
> c) hard
> d) fitness

PART 3 (10:30:00–11:53:00)

6 Play Part 3. Tell the students to put the sentences in the correct order.

a) 2   b) 7   c) 6   d) 3   e) 5   f) 8   g) 4   h) 1

If there is time, let the students watch the complete unit at the end so they can enjoy the whole film.

After you watch

7 Put the students into pairs and ask them to discuss the questions. You may need to help them with the vocabulary of each sport, e.g. football pitch, baseball bat, badminton racquet, tennis court.

Optional extension

Ask the different pairs for the names of the sports they discussed and write them on the board. If most pairs were talking about the same sport then ask the students to give you the names of some other sports as well.

Put the students into groups. Ask them to write as many comparative and superlative sentences about the different sports as they can in five minutes, e.g *Football is more popular than cricket. Cricket matches are longer than tennis matches. Footballers are fitter than people who do horse riding.* Tell them that this is a competition and they'll get more points if the sentences are grammatically and factually correct.

If the students run out of ideas, prompt them with the following adjectives: *fit, fast, long, exciting, popular, big, small.*

After five minutes, ask groups to read out their sentences and award a point for each sentence that has a correct comparative or superlative. Award another point for each sentence that is factually correct. The group with the most points at the end is the winner.

4 A new star

(N = Narrator; S = Steve; I = Interviewer;
D = Damien; M = Man)

PART 1

N: Cricket is a game with a long history. It goes back to the 13th century, but we don't know how they played it then. The modern game started in England in the 1700s. There are eleven players in each team. The rules are quite complicated, but the team with the most runs, or points, wins. Although it's never been popular in Scotland or Wales, today cricket is a global sport. It's watched and played by millions, from Australia to Pakistan, and from South Africa to the West Indies. Cricket's now even played in the USA and is popular with all ages, and not only boys.

The cathedral city of Worcester is the home of one of England's most famous and successful teams. Worcester County Cricket Club was founded in 1865. The club has one of the most attractive grounds in the country. Its pavilion hasn't changed since 1898. In the past, cricket was the relaxed game of gentlemen. Today it's a highly competitive sport for professional players.

These players have to be as fit as professional footballers. And cricketers have to play for a lot longer than other sportsmen. Games can last one, four or even five days so the players have to be in great physical shape, and never lose their concentration.

This is the Worcester Academy team. Teenage players who all have a special talent for the game. They train hard, play hard, and achieve a high level of physical fitness. But how do young people become top class, professional players?

PART 2

N: Steve Davis is one of the stars of the Academy team.

S: I've been playing cricket since I was six, so I've been playing for about twelve years now and I'm still enjoying it.

N: Steve has a natural talent for the game, and he's also ambitious!

S: I would really love to play for England. As soon as I started playing it was my number one goal.

I: What's it like as a trainee? Describe a typical week.

S: We get a weekly programme sent to us every Friday. We'd either have a game, it can either be a one day game, a two day game or a three day game. And then on the other days we usually have training.

I: How often do you train?

S: Um, we train most days really.

D: You've got to chase it. And that's ten more please, you two at the end.

M: The winners of the county final goes to …

N: Today, Steve is giving a prize for a local schools' cricket competition.

I: Do you have to be very fit to play well?

S: Um, you have to be incredibly fit to play, to play cricket. And because the game's getting quicker and faster, then, you know, your fitness is really important.

I: What do you love about cricket?

S: I love everything about cricket. I love the physical side of it. I love coming training and working really hard. I love the fitness side of it. I love it all.

PART 3

D: Played, Stevie. So just watch your head, right. Because, you're just, as he's, as he's coming in you're just dropping, but I want it still and level. OK?

N: Damien D'Oliveira is the director and assistant coach of the academy team.

D: I was originally taken on by Worcester as a professional player, and I played as a professional cricketer from 1982 to 1996.

I: What's the best thing about being a coach?

D: Identifying young talent, working with them, helping them develop, watching them develop, watching them improve. Hopefully getting them into your first team, and the ultimate goal would be to get them to play for England.

I: How fit do the players have to be?

D: The fitness of the players nowadays is probably 100% more than it used to be. Er, here at Worcester we employ full-time a fitness instructor.

I: What are Steve's best points as a player?

D: He's obviously very talented at the job that he does, ie, batting and wicket-keeping. He moves well, he's got a very good pair of hands, and has got all the makings of a top-class player.

Photocopiable

7 A bad day

Summary

This video unit could be used as support to materials in unit 7 of the Student's Book after the reading section. It is a drama about an office worker who comes back from holiday and has a disastrous day at work.

Language focus

Grammar: past simple and present perfect

Vocabulary and expressions: *accounts, department, e-mail, keyboard, manager, meeting, office, reception, sales figures, screen, security pass, temporary pass*

Procedure

Before you watch

1 Put the students into pairs and tell them to put the words in the box under the correct headings. Check the answers and give the students the chance to ask for clarification of any new words.

> **Place:** office   reception
> **Office equipment:** desk   screen   keyboard
> **Document:** sales figures   e-mail
> **Person:** manager   boss   receptionist
> **Other:** security pass   meeting

2 Put the students into pairs and tell them to do the activity. Encourage them to give reasons for their choices and negotiate with each other. The answers are up to the students.

Ask the students to remain in pairs and discuss which of the things in the list they have done. If they still go to school, you could change *meeting* to *lesson*, *colleagues* to *school mates*, and *security pass* to *timetable*.

3 Tell the students to read the sentences and discuss what they think happens in Jack's day. Tell the students not to worry about who says the sentences at the moment. At this point there are no right or wrong answers.

While you watch

4 Play the video. Ask the students to identify who says the lines.

Play the video again and tell them to ask for the video to be paused when the lines are said.

> a) Receptionist
> b) Jack
> c) Jack
> d) Jack
> e) Nina
> f) Nina
> g) Nina
> h) Nina

5 Play the video again and ask the students to put the scenes in order.

> a) 4   b) 3   c) 1   d) 2   e) 6   f) 5

If there is time, let the students watch the complete unit at the end so they can enjoy the whole film.

After you watch

6 Tell the students to match the parts of the story with the photos.

> 1) d
> 2) b
> 3) e
> 4) f
> 5) c
> 6) a

7 Ask the students to complete the sentences. Then discuss the usage of the sentences.

> a) disturb
> b) terribly
> c) sure
> d) yet
> e) take
> f) believe

> a) is a polite way of disturbing someone.
> b) is a polite way of apologising.
> c) is a checking question. As it questions someone's performance it needs to be said politely.
> d) is a checking question. As it questions someone's performance it needs to be said politely.
> e) is an informal and impatient way of asking someone to hurry up.
> f) is an exclamation of frustration about a situation.

8 Put the students into groups and tell them to discuss the questions. Encourage them to think about who is responsible for each action and give reasons. Answers are dependent on the students' opinions. The following are opinions that can be supported by evidence.

a) Was the receptionist too hard on Jack? Why/why not?

No, she was just following the regulations. Yes, she was a little inflexible and unfriendly, but perhaps Jack's attitude made her angry.

b) Did Jack arrange a meeting with the accounts department?

It's not clear from the video but Jack's answer seemed a little unsure. It seems odd that he can't find the e-mail he said he sent. Perhaps he never sent one.

c) Were the wrong sales figures Jack's or Nina's fault? Why?

This was clearly Jack's fault. Nina said Australia. He was distracted and tired and didn't listen properly.

d) Was the picture of Nina on Jack's screen his fault? Why/why not?

Not really. A colleague sent it. But he wanted to look at it. If workers are sending pictures like that perhaps Nina isn't managing her team very well.

e) Do you think Nina should have behaved differently towards Jack? How?

No. Jack was late. Perhaps he has had similar problems in the past.

Yes. Jack's flight was late, so it wasn't totally his fault. Nina could have talked to him and showed she cared. Giving him orders just

7 A bad day

(R = Receptionist; J = Jack; N = Nina; K = Kim)

R: Excuse me, have you got your security pass?
J: Sorry?
R: Can I see your security pass, please?
J: Ah … no. I'm afraid not. It's in my other suit.
R: Then I'm afraid you can't go in.
J: Yeah, I'm a bit late this morning. I've been away on holiday and only got back last night – my flight was delayed.
R: I'm sorry, but it's the new regulation. What's your name?
J: Jack … Jack Brown.
R: And who's your manager?
J: Nina Miles. No, don't call her … I'm really rather late.
R: Oh, hello. Sorry to disturb you. I have a Jack Brown in Reception. Yes, apparently his flight was delayed. OK. Here's your temporary pass.
J: Thank you.

N: Good morning, Jack.
J: Nina, I'm terribly sorry, I tried to call …
N: I haven't got time for explanations. Did you arrange this morning's meeting before you left for your holiday?
J: Meeting?
N: With the Accounts Department.
J: Oh, yes.
N: It's extremely important.
J: Oh, don't worry. I fixed everything. It's for eleven o'clock.
N: That's in ten minutes.
J: Oh, yes, of course. You see, my plane arrived terribly late.
N: So did you.

J: Jack Brown. Yes Nina, I'm coming.
N: So, did you have a nice holiday?
J: Yes, it was lovely.
N: Where did you go?
J: South of France. The weather was fantastic. We went swimming in the sea every day and er … we had a swimming pool, too …
N: It's half past eleven. They're not coming, are they?

J: Maybe not.
N: Are you sure you invited them?
J: Of course I did. I sent an e-mail and …
N: Could you show me a copy of your e-mail, please? In my office after lunch.
J: No problem.

J: Jack Brown.
N: Have you found that e-mail yet?
J: Not yet, I'm still looking for it.
N: Well, don't take all day. And can you get me the Australian sales figures?
J: Sure.
K: Hi Jack! Butter-fingers.
J: Oh no!
K: I'll see you later.

N: Come in! Have you brought that e-mail, Jack?
J: Er, no, Nina. But I've got the sales figures.
N: What are these?
J: The sales figures for Austria.
N: I can't believe this, Jack. I asked for the sales figures for Australia!
J: Oh. Sorry!

N: Jack.
J: Nina!
N: Have you finished those sales figures?
J: Nearly.
N: And have you found that e-mail for the meeting?
J: I'm sorry, Nina. I think I deleted it by mistake.
N: You haven't had a good day, have you, Jack?
J: Not really.
N: Well, I'm going home now. Could you leave the figures on my desk before you leave?
J: Absolutely.
N: What is it?
J: What?
N: On your screen.
J: Nothing.
N: Could you move? Move, Jack!
J: Nina … Er …

9 *Schooldays*

Summary

This video unit could be used as support to materials in unit 9 of the Student's Book in the following places:

- after the *Close Up* activity to follow the reading text *Schooldays of a Rock Star* on page 55.
- after the students have given their anecdote (on page 57), as a model for comparison.

It is a documentary about two generations of a family from a village in the Midlands, in the centre of England. The parents went to the same school as their children.

Language focus

Grammar: present simple and past simple; modal structures: obligation and permission

Vocabulary and expressions: *cane, cap, chew gum, detention, dressmaking, homework, lines, punishment, ruler, school rules, school uniform, shorthand and typing, slipper*

Background information

Comprehensive schools were introduced in the UK about the time the parents in this video went to secondary school. The comprehensive school system was based on the principle that children of all abilities could study together in the same school (and often in the same class). The main differences between the parents' experience of education and that of their children is in the range of school subjects, the specialisation of boys and girls into different subjects, and the approach to discipline. For example, Gillian talks about studying shorthand and typing and dressmaking. These two subjects were considered necessary to prepare girls both for secretarial work and home-making. Now boys and girls all study the same subjects.

Language notes

Would occurs when the adults talk about their past experiences. It is used to talk about habitual actions in the past.

Shorthand was more commonly used in the past. It is a written code used by secretaries and journalists to transcribe dictated letters and interviews. They can then write up the text in full later on.

Ruler, slipper, cane are all forms of corporal punishment that were used in the past. In Britain today, physical punishment has been abolished in schools.

Lines is a form of punishment where the student has to write the same sentence many times.

Yellow sheet is a written warning from the teacher. It's yellow to show the seriousness of the offence.

Detention is a common form of punishment in modern British schools. Students have to stay in a classroom under supervision for a fixed period of time, usually after school.

Procedure

Before you watch

1 Put the students into groups and tell them to discuss the questions. If there is a mix of ages in the class, put different aged students in groups.

While you watch

PART 1 (17:40:00–18:48:00)

2 Play Part 1 and tell the students to complete the family tree with the names in the box and the ages of the children.

> a) John
> b) Pauline
> c) Tom
> d) Connie
> e) 14
> f) 12
> g) 14
> h) 12

Optional extension

To provide practice of family vocabulary ask the students to answer the following questions.

a) Which two of the adults are related by birth?

b) What are the relationships between the eight members of the two families?

Example: Claire is Gillian's <u>daughter</u>.

1) Gillian is Tom's _____ and Luke and Connie's _____ .

2) Jeff is Connie's _____ and Tom and Claire's _____ .

3) Tom is Claire's _____ .

4) Connie is Luke's _____ .

5) Luke is Jeff's _____ .

6) Tom and Luke are _____ .

7) John is Gillian's _____ and Pauline's _____ .

8) Pauline is Jeff's _____ and John's _____ .

Play Part 1 again if necessary so that they can check their answers.

a) John and Jeff. They are brothers.
b) 1) mother; aunt
   2) father; uncle
   3) brother
   4) sister
   5) son
   6) cousins
   7) husband; brother-in-law
   8) wife; sister-in-law

PART 2 (18:49:00–20:47:00)

3 Give the students a few minutes to read through the statements. Then play Part 2 and tell the students to decide whether the statements are true or false. You could ask them to try and correct any false statements.

a) T
b) F (she did like her)
c) F (it's PE)
d) T
e) F (Connie doesn't study dressmaking or shorthand and typing. However, she does study modern languages, geography and sport which Gillian didn't study.)
f) T
g) T
h) T

Optional extension

Put the students into groups. Ask them to discuss the following questions.

a) What is your favourite subject? Why?
b) Do you study all the same subjects as Gillian and Connie?
c) If not, what are the differences?
d) Are there any subjects that you have to study?
e) Is there any subject that you don't study but would like to?
f) Who is your favourite teacher? Why?

After a few minutes, ask one student from each group to talk to the class about their discussions. You could do a class survey for questions a, e and f, to see how many students have the same answers.

PART 3 (20:48:00–22:19:00)

4 Ask the students to read the text and complete the school rules using the words in the box.

Ask the students to watch Part 3 and check their answers.

a) stand   b) smoking; walk   c) wear
d) gum   e) arrive; uniform   f) hit
g) lines   h) move; ring   i) hour's

PART 4 (22:20:00–24:00:00)

5 Before watching Part 4, ask the students to read the sentences and guess the correct options. Then play the video and tell the students to check their answers.

a) enjoyed
b) fast
c) had to
d) have to
e) can sometimes
f) will probably

If there is time, let the students watch the complete unit at the end so they can enjoy the whole film.

After you watch

6 Put the students into pairs and ask them to say what is similar and different in the parents' and children's experience of school.

Possible answers:
Differences: punishments, meals, school subjects, school rules
Similarities: homework, uniforms

7 Put the students into groups and ask them to compare their own experiences with the people in the video. Offer them examples from your own schooldays.

9 Schooldays

(N = Narrator; I = Interviewer; J = Jeff;
Jo = John; P = Pauline; G = Gillian; T = Tom;
L = Luke; C = Claire; Co = Connie)

PART 1

N: The beautiful village of Helmdon is in the Midlands, in the heart of England. People have lived here for generations and many of them work on farms. It's a small community with a church and a pub. This is Tom and his sister, Claire. And this is Luke, and his sister, Connie. The boys are fourteen and the girls are twelve. They all go to Magdalene College School, which is just outside the village.
And these are Tom and Claire's parents, Gillian and John. And John's brother Geoff, and his wife Pauline, who are Luke and Connie's parents. And all the parents went to the Magdalene College School too.

PART 2

What do the children think about their school, and how has it changed since their parents were there?
I: What was your favourite subject at school?
G: History.
I: Why?
G: Because I enjoyed it the most. I found it the most interesting.
Jo: History. Because I liked the teacher.
P: Typing and shorthand, because I had a lovely teacher. She made it very enjoyable.
J: Mathematics. Because I enjoyed it.
T: PE. I like sport.
C: English.
L: Music. I like playing the guitar.
Co: Art. Because I'm probably the best at art and I like drawing.

I: What subjects did you study?
G: English, English language and English literature, history, science, maths, dressmaking, shorthand and typing.
Co: Maths, English, modern languages, science, geography, history, sport, and I can't think of any others.

I: Do you like your teachers?
Co: Some are OK, but some are just really horrible.
L: Yeah, I like them. They're cool.

I: Who was your favourite teacher?
J: My French teacher.
I: Why?
J: Because he only had one arm and I admired him as a man.
Jo: Mr Beresford.
I: Why?
Jo: Because he was a very good teacher.
I: Who's your favourite teacher?
C: I don't really have a favourite teacher!
L: Mr Blunsdon.
I: Why?
L: Because he teaches my favourite subject.
I: Which is?
L: Music.
Co: My RE teacher because he's fun and he's really nice as well.

PART 3

I: What were the school rules like?
G: You had to stand up as soon as the teacher came into the room, and again when they left.
P: No smoking. No alcohol on the premises. Um, do not run, always walk.
J: You had to wear your cap from the moment you left your home in the morning until the moment you got home at night.
C: You're not allowed to, like, chew gum. Um, you've got to obey the teachers.
Co: You have to arrive on time with everything you need. And no running, pushing. Um, no chewing gum, and you have to wear set school uniform.
I: What were the punishments?
P: The punishments were more physical than they are today. A teacher would shout at you, maybe even hit you. If you'd behaved really badly you'd be sent to the Head and you'd get a ruler over the palm of your hand.
J: You were given lines or you had the slipper, or you had the cane.
Co: They'll tell you off and then they might move you and then yellow sheet, then breaktime detention, lunchtime detention, then after school detention, then they might ring home.
I: Did you have to do homework?
Jo: Yes, we did. About 90 minutes.
T: Yes, you do have to do your homework. If you don't, you'll get a detention. You're meant to do an hour's homework every night.

PART 4

I: What were your school dinners like?

Jo: Excellent.

I: What did they consist of?

Jo: A meat and two veg, followed by a pudding.

P: Delicious. They were very traditional: potato, meat pie and a nice pudding.

C: You can get stuff like chips, burgers, hotdogs, sometimes pasta or sausages or baked beans.

I: Did you have to wear a school uniform?

P: Yes, I did. The summer uniform was a blue cotton dress.

J: Yes, we did. Black shoes, black socks, black trousers, grey shirt, tie, black jacket and a cap.

T: You have to wear a school uniform all year round. It's quite nice in the summer because it's no ties and you're sometimes allowed to wear trainers.

Co: In the winter you wear black trousers with a shirt and tie and school jumper. And in the summer you wear black trousers, or girls can wear a skirt and polo shirt. And then if you get cold, a school jumper.

I: Do you think your children will go to the same school?

T: Yes, I think they will.

C: Maybe.

L: I'd like them to, considering I've been and my parents have been, so, yeah. It would be cool.

Co: I don't know. Um, if we live near here, then, yeah.

12 Confessions

Summary

This video unit could be used as support to materials in unit 12 of the Student's Book in the following places:

- before the anecdote on page 73 to enrich the students' vocabulary and act as a model.
- after the students have given their anecdote, as a model for comparison.

These are monologues of genuine unscripted memories of naughty childhood behaviour.

Language focus

Grammar: past simple for narrative

Note: One speaker uses *used to* but it is not necessary to focus on this in the lesson unless your class is already very confident in the past simple, and you feel they would be able to use it in their own storytelling.

Background information

Matt is from the USA and uses American English lexical items. These are pre-taught in exercise 1.

Procedure

Before you watch

1 The following words appear in the confessions the students are going to hear. Ask them to match the words and the definitions. If dictionaries are available, the students may find them useful.

a) 7	b) 9	c) 4	d) 2	e) 3	f) 8
g) 5	h) 10	i) 6	j) 1		

While you watch

2 Ask the students to look at the pictures and describe them. Elicit *scissors*, *snowball*, *nail varnish*, *stick* and *plum*. Ask the students to predict what the naughty children did.

Tell the students they're going to watch some people telling stories about their childhood. Play the whole video unit and tell the students to match the people and the illustrations by writing the relevant letter in each box.

1	d
2	b
3	e
4	a
5	c

3 Put the students into pairs. Tell them to work together and answer the questions.

4 Ask the students to read through the questions. Then play the video and tell them to answer the questions and check their answers to exercise 3.

3
a) Joanne and Nicola
b) Joseph
c) Nicola
d) Darina's
e) Nicola
f) Matthew

4
a) 1
b) 2
c) 2
d) 3
e) 1
f) 3
g) 2
h) 1

If there is time, let the students watch the complete unit at the end so they can enjoy the whole film.

After you watch

5 Put the students into groups. Ask them to discuss the five confessions and decide which one they think is the most serious, i.e. the naughtiest.

6 Go through the phrases with the students. If necessary, play the video again and ask them to call out when they hear the expressions. Then ask the students to tell their partner their own childhood stories. They can tell positive or exciting stories instead of anecdotes about when they were naughty if they prefer.

12 Confessions

(D = Darina; Jo = Joanne; J = Joseph;
N = Nicola; M = Matthew)

D: Um, this is a story from when I was about five years old. Um, I had a friend who lived next door, and one day we were playing in my room and we decided to make a scientific concoction, a scientific, um, experiment. So we took all of my mother's shampoos and nail varnishes and perfumes, and we poured them all into the bath. She came in about half an hour later and went absolutely crazy. She sent my friend home and I wasn't allowed to go out for a whole week afterwards.

Jo: When I was younger, my sister and I had dolls. We're twins and we both loved our dolls. One day, when Kim went to school, she left her doll, and I decided to cut the hair off her doll with a pair of scissors. When she came back from school she was very angry and she didn't speak to me for months.

J: Well, when I was young I used to live in a road with several other children who lived around. And there was a friend across the road called David, who had a big plum tree in his garden. Lots of big, fat, juicy plums used to come every year. And, er, we quickly found out that if you put one of these plums on a stick, you could throw the plum quite a long way, and quite hard. Um, anyway, also in the road where I lived there was an old man who was always complaining about us cycling on the pavement and just generally making a noise, like children do. Er, I don't think he liked children very much. Anyway, one day we went over to his house when he was out, and we got lots and lots of plums with our sticks and threw them at his windows, and all his windows were covered in plums and plum juice and it was a big mess. Um, and this was revenge for us, for him telling us off all the time. Anyway, it was a silly idea because we lived about a hundred yards away from this man, and he came out of his house one day when my father was there and he told him, and my father took me inside and told me off.

N: It was when we were living in this house in London and my parents had painted the wall in my sister and my bedroom, and my sister had just learnt to write. And I wrote her name on the wall in her handwriting so that my parents thought that she'd done it. And she got into trouble with my parents. My mother was very angry. And I never told anybody that I did it.

M: I remember one winter there was a lot of snow and my friends and I decided to make some snowballs. But this time we made them extra special because we put rocks in the snowballs. And then we decided that we would throw the snowballs at the passing cars at the road nearby. And, um, we threw snowballs at one car in particular and it broke the window of the car. The guy pulled over, got out of his car, and he started chasing us. And we ran, had to hop fences and go through neighbours' backyards and finally we got away.

14 *The audition*

Summary

This video unit could be used as support to materials in unit 14 of the Student's Book after *Telephone Talk* on page 85. It is a drama about an actor who is trying to get to an audition.

Language focus

Grammar: indirect questions, offers and requests

Vocabulary and expressions: *Can I call you back?, Can you speak up?, Could I speak to … ?, Hold on a minute … , I'm afraid … , I'm calling from … , You've got the wrong number …*

Background information

An audition is an interview for a role in a play or a film. Actors, singers and dancers perform in front of the director and casting director. Actors can be asked to perform some of the dialogue from the production to see if they are suitable for the part.

Steven Spielberg is the film director of some of the most successful films ever made. His films include: *AI, Catch me if you can, ET, Jurassic Park, the Indiana Jones* trilogy, *Minority Report,* and *Schindler's List.*

Procedure

Before you watch

1   Ask the students to make notes about the questions and to ask if they need help with vocabulary.

2   Ask the students to work with a partner. Ask them to discuss their films. Suggest they ask each other questions about their films or if they both know the film to compare their opinions of it. Ask some students to tell the whole class about their film.

🔲 While you watch

3   Ask the students if they have heard about Steven Spielberg. Have a short discussion about his films. Ask them how they think an actor would feel if he were asked to act in a Spielberg film. Tell the students that they are going to see a short drama. Go through the sentences with the students. Then play the video and ask the students to circle the correct options.

a) Alex King
b) an actor
c) Ealing Studios
d) an audition
e) happy; excited
f) depressed
g) doesn't

4   Put the students into pairs. Ask them to read through the parts of the story and put them in order. Tell them to use a pencil so they can correct their answers if they change their minds.

5   Ask the students to say what order they think is correct. Allow the class to debate the parts of the story if they disagree. Put the suggested order on the board. Play the video again and ask the students to check their answers.

a) 2	b) 6	c) 3	d) 8
e) 7	f) 4	g) 5	h) 1

If there is time, let the students watch the complete unit at the end so they can enjoy the whole film.

After you watch

6   Ask the students to complete the phone conversations from the video using the words in the box. Play the video again for them to check if necessary (29:18:00–30:45:00).

a) speak	b) sorry
c) ringing	d) wondering
e) I'll	f) It's
g) afraid	h) breaking
i) hear	j) saying

7   Ask the students to work in pairs. Tell them to take a few minutes to choose two situations and write two telephone conversations. Then ask them to practise saying their conversations. If necessary, provide them with some prompts. For example: *Hello. Could I speak to … ?; Hello. I'd like to book a cab.; I'm afriad you've got the wrong number.*

14 The audition

(A = Alex King; S = Sarah; W1 = Woman 1;
W2 = Woman 2; D = David; M = Man;
Sp = Mr Spielberg)

A: ... It's a fantastic opportunity. A really big film. A blockbuster.

S: And is he going to be there?

A: Oh yeah. Steven Spielberg, the man himself. He's at the studios now.

S: That's amazing.

A: Listen, can you call me back? I've just got to call a cab.

S: Sure, go ahead.

W1: 1, 2, 3 Taxis.

A: Hello. Can I have a cab for ... Belsize Park, please? I'm outside the delicatessen.

W1: What name, please?

A: King. Alex King.

W1: And where are you going?

A: To Ealing Studios.

W1: Is that the film studios?

A: That's right.

W1: And when would you like it?

A: As soon as you can. I've got a very important appointment.

W1: OK, I'll just check to see if we have any cabs in your area.

W1: Mr King?

A: Yeah?

W1: It'll be five minutes. Moscow 205.

A: OK, but don't be late, I don't have much ... time.

A: Hello, Sarah.

S: So you're really going to meet Steven Spielberg?

A: Uh huh. He's attending all the auditions. I'm in the running for the main character.

S: When's your audition?

A: In ... an hour.

S: Where are you now?

A: Don't worry. It only takes 45 minutes to get there ... Hold on, I've got another call. I'll get back to you. Hello?

D: Could I speak to Alex Keen, please?

A: King.

D: I'm sorry?

A: It's King. Alex King. You said Keen.

D: Oh, I'm sorry, Mr King. My name's David Antonucci. I'm ringing from Ealing Studios on behalf of Mr Spielberg.

A: Oh, right.

D: I was wondering if you could be here a quarter of an hour earlier? Mr Spielberg has another engagement and then he has to leave immediately for the airport.

A: No problem. I'll be there. I wouldn't miss this for the world.

D: Thank you very much. We'll see you soon then. Goodbye.

A: Bye.

A: Come on, come on ...

M: Hello?

A: 1, 2, 3 Taxis?

M: Er, no. I'm afraid you've got the wrong number.

A: Right.

W1: 1, 2, 3 Taxis.

A: Hello, it's Alex King. I booked a cab over ten minutes ago ...

W1: We're doing all we can, Sir, but I'm afraid we're rather busy this afternoon. A cab should be with you ...

A: Can you speak up? I can't ...

W1: ... the cab should ... in about ...

A: Hold on you're breaking up. Hello?

W1: Can you hear me now?

A: Yeah, yeah, yeah.

W1: I was just saying that the cab should be with you any minute now.

A: You're sure? This is very urgent.

W1: We're doing everything we can, Sir.

A: Wait a minute!

W2: Ever Ready Cabs?

A: Hello, can I have a cab for Belsize Park, please, it's urgent.

W2: No problem, Sir. We can have a car with you in just ... fifteen minutes.

D: Hello.

A: Hello, David, this is …

D: This is David Antonucci. I can't take your call at the moment. Please leave your name and number and speak after the beep.

A: Hello, David? This is Alex King. Could you possibly call me back. Please? Thank you.

A: Hello.

D: Alex? Hi. I got your message. I think it would be better if you spoke to Mr Spielberg directly.

A: Directly?

D: In person. Is that OK?

A: Oh yes, absolutely. That's … cool.

D: Excellent. Mr Spielberg?

Sp: Hello?

A: Mr Spielberg? This is Alex … Alex King.

17 *My humans*

Summary

This video unit could be used to support material in unit 17 of the Student's Book in the following places:

- after the *Special Friends* section on page 103 to follow the listening and give students a different perspective.
- after the Language Reference on page 104.

It is a drama about a dog and his humans seen from the viewpoint of the dog.

Language focus

Grammar: present simple for routine; expressions of preference

Vocabulary: personality adjectives; *kind, energetic, intelligent, lazy, naughty, loyal, independent* expressions: *to get on well with (someone), to be interested in, to be keen on (something), to make decisions, to worry about*

Background information

The British are famous for their love of animals and they certainly keep a lot of pets – seven million people own a dog and eight million own a cat. Pet owners spend a massive amount of money on pet food, equipment and vets' bills. There are many people who breed and show their animals. One particular dog show, Crufts, which is held in London, is famous in the UK, and is even covered on British TV. Other contests that are popular are those showing working dogs such as sheep dogs, which are used in the UK to help look after sheep.

Unfortunately, not everyone in the UK is kind to animals, and there are many organisations such as the RSPCA (Royal Society for the Prevention of Cruelty to Animals) that protect animals and campaign for changes to the law. There are also dogs' and cats' homes, such as the famous Battersea Dogs' Home in London, where people can go and choose a new pet from the abandoned animals that are kept there.

Most British people treat their pets as part of the family and keep them in the house, even allowing them to sleep on beds and sofas. However, some things are changing. In many parks nowadays dog owners are legally obliged to clear up the mess that their dog makes.

Procedure

Before you watch

1 As a warm up, ask the students to talk briefly about their pets if they have any. Then put them into pairs and tell them to look at the picture. Ask them to guess which adjectives apply to each character. This is a speculative exercise and there are no right or wrong answers.

▭ While you watch

2 Tell the students to look at the pictures and describe them before watching. Then play the video and ask them to put the pictures in order.

> a) 2   b) 6   c) 5   d) 3   e) 1   f) 4

3 Tell the students to read the sentences and see if they can remember who Bruno is talking about.

4 Ask the students to say what Bruno is like. Is he intellectual/active/intelligent/healthy/loving etc? Then ask them to look at the opinions and try to remember which ones are right and which are wrong. Ask the students to correct the wrong opinions.

5 Tell the students to watch the video again and check their answers to exercises 3 and 4. Then check the answers as a class.

> **3**
>
> | | | |
> |---|---|---|
> | a) Alice | b) Bob | c) Alice |
> | d) Bruno | e) Bruno | f) Candy |
> | g) Bruno | h) Bob | i) Alice |
>
> **4**
> a) ✓
> b) ✓
> c) Wrong. It isn't always easy living with humans.
> d) Wrong. I've never been interested in philosophical questions.
> e) Wrong. I'm a dog of actions, not words.
> f) ✓
> g) ✓
> h) Wrong. I prefer sleeping on the bed.
> i) ✓

If there is time, let the students watch the complete unit at the end so they can enjoy the whole film.

After you watch

6 Ask the students to think about their daily life and complete the sentences. Then put them in pairs and tell them to compare their opinions.

7 Ask the students to complete the sentences. If there is time, play the video again for them to check their answers. Tell them to call out when they hear the sentences.

a) positive attitude	b) Unfortunately
c) on the whole	d) worry about
e) main problem	f) I suppose

8 This exercise can be done as homework if there isn't time in class.

17 My humans

(B = Bruno; A = Alice; Bo = Bob; C = Candy)

B: Hi. My name's Bruno. I'm a collie. And these are my humans, Bob and Alice. They're both in their thirties – which is still quite young for humans. They're kind and have nice personalities, although I don't think they're very intelligent. Alice has got a very positive attitude to life, she laughs a lot and she, erm, she gives me unconditional love. Which is nice. Bob often does silly things that make me smile. He isn't very independent – Alice makes all the big decisions – and, er, I suppose he's a bit lazy. But he's a good companion. It isn't always easy living with humans, but on the whole, we get on very well.

B: Bob doesn't take much exercise. I often worry about him because he's not very fit. I'm keen on running but with Bob I have to go quite slowly. It's a drag, really. It's better in the park, though. He takes off my lead so I can run around. The park's really cool. I sometimes meet up with friends here. I like an Afghan that lives near here. Her name's Candy. When we meet up we often have a chat. She's quite intellectual and just loves asking difficult questions.

C: If you were a famous human being, what famous human being would you like to be?

B: Um … I don't know, really.

C: If you were an animal, what animal would you like to be?

B: Um … a dog.

C: If you were a car, what car would you like to be?

B: Um … a blue one?

C: Intriguing.

B: I've never been interested in philosophical questions. I prefer doing things. You know, like chasing cats or barking at the postman. I'm a dog of action, not words.

Bo: Good boy, you're a good boy! Yes, a good boy.

A: Here you are, Bruno.

B: My humans nearly always give me tinned food. It isn't very attractive, is it? I've never been keen on convenience food. It all tastes the same really. But the main problem is, it's not very good for you.

A: What's the matter, Bruno? Aren't you hungry?

B: I try to keep in good condition but it's not easy. If I could go out on my own it would be fine. But, well, I have to go out with Bob, and Bob doesn't like running. I suppose I worry about it a bit because your health's the most important thing, really.

A: Would you like some biscuits, Bruno? Come on. Eat up your dinner. OK. OK. Come on eat up your dinner. Look, eat up your dinner. Go on! Come on!

B: I do like biscuits, though. They're not organic but they've got a lovely flavour. And they're really crunchy.

B: In the afternoons, I enjoy a little nap. I have a dog basket with an old blanket but I don't find it very comfortable. I prefer sleeping on their bed. Unfortunately, Alice disapproves of this.

A: Bruno! How many times have I told you? Get down!

B: I hate it when humans keep you awake during the day.

Bo: He's a good dog, Bruno.

A: He's no trouble at all.

Bo: No … I just have to take him for walks … but that's all right, really. It gets me out the house.

A: He's very loyal.

Bo: Oh yes, dogs are loyal. Man's best friend. Not like cats.

A: No, although cats are more intelligent.

Bo: Probably.

A: I don't think Bruno thinks a lot.

Bo: Bruno? No.

B: I really think Candy fancies me. The next time she asks me one of those questions, I'm going to say something really clever. Something philosophical. Like, um, if I were a famous human, what human would I like to be? And my answer? Einstein … or maybe Leonardo da Vinci. Yeah. That'll surprise her.

Summary

This video unit can be used as support to materials in unit 18 of the Student's Book after *The mother of all circles* listening on page 107. It is a documentary about the crop-circle phenomena.

Language focus

Grammar: past tenses, passives

Vocabulary: adjectives; *amazing, calming, enigmatic, extraordinary, incredible, ingenious, magnetic*

nouns; *civilisation, detail, effect, equipment, form, shape, work*

Background information

Unit 18 gives a lot of information about crop circles. The video builds on that background and allows the students to actually see a lot of different formations.

Procedure

Before you watch

1 Ask the students to look at the photos and tell you anything they can about them. Make sure they all know that Stonehenge (the photo in the bottom right corner) is a stone circle built around 4,500 years ago and situated in the south of England.

Put the students into groups. Ask them to look at the questions and discuss them. Tell them they can use the words in the box to help them, as well as their own ideas. Clarify that 'croppies' refers to the people who study crop circles. After a few minutes, ask some students from each group to tell the rest of the class about their discussions.

🔘 While you watch

2 Tell the students to read the sentences and guess the order before they watch the video. Play the video and tell the students to check their sentences are in the correct order.

> a) 2
> b) 6
> c) 4
> d) 5
> e) 3
> f) 1

3 Ask the students to read the questions and try to answer them without watching the video.

4 Put the students into pairs. Ask the students to complete the text using some of the words in the box. Clarify that not all the words in the box need to be used.

5 Ask the students to watch the video again and check their answers to exercises 3 and 4. The answers to exercise 4 can be found between 41:48:00 and 42:17:00.

> **3**
> a) 2
> b) 3
> c) 1
> d) 2
> e) 1
> f) 3
>
> **4**
> a) civilisations
> b) ancient
> c) alien
> d) magnetic

If there is time, let the students watch the complete unit at the end so they can enjoy the whole film.

After you watch

6 Put the students in groups and ask them to discuss the questions. Ask the same groups to tell the whole class about their discussions.

18 Crop circles

In the south of England, in the heart of the countryside, we can see signs of earlier civilisations. There's the man-made construction of Silbury Hill, the largest prehistoric earthwork in Europe. And there are the great stone circles of Avebury built, like Stonehenge, over four and a half thousand years ago. Why these monuments were built is still a mystery today. But in recent years, new shapes have appeared in this landscape as strange as those ancient monuments – crop circles.

They are created mysteriously overnight, and in the morning, farmers wake up to discover these beautiful, enigmatic shapes in their fields. Since 1980, when the first crop circle was reported, these amazing forms have appeared every year. Each one is different, and they're beautiful works of art. But do they have a meaning? And who – or what – makes them?

It's hardly surprising that 'croppies', people who study crop circles, become obsessed with these extraordinary works. And they can have a profound effect on the people who visit them. On the ground, you can't see the size and patterns so clearly … but these crop patterns have a calming effect. They encourage you to stop, to look, to listen – perhaps even to meditate. And on the ground, you can see some incredible details … such as these knots at the centre of the patterns.

Some farmers are upset at losing their crops. However, others are more sympathetic … and visitors are encouraged to give a donation when they visit the sites.

To get a better view of the circles, film makers have invented some ingenious equipment. They attach the video camera to long, light poles and look at the images through video glasses.

Many people believe that the aim of the circle-makers is to make us all more aware of earlier civilisations. The crop circles are a kind of symbolic language. For them, it's no coincidence that so many crop circles are located close to ancient sites. Some think they are an alien communication. Others believe they are created by the earth's magnetic energies. Who's right? Who can say? But the mystery and the beauty of these crop circles remains.

NYC subway centenary

1. Read the text.

2004 marked the 100th anniversary of one of the greatest feats of engineering in the world. In October, New York City hosted a number of events to celebrate the opening of the underground system one hundred years previously, in 1904.

When the New York City subway opened in 1904, fares were just 5 cents. They remained at that price until 1948, when they were raised to 10 cents. Now it costs $2 for one ride or $4 for a 24-hour unlimited ride card.

On its opening day in 1904, there were 14 km of track. Today there are 1,355 km of track with 1,062 km of them currently in use.

Although there are 468 subway stations, only 277 of them are underground. Many stations are above the ground. The highest subway line is in Brooklyn. It's 27 m above street level and offers some beautiful views over the city. The longest stretch of line is 52 km long. It runs from the centre of Manhattan out to the borough of Queen's. Back underground, the deepest subway line runs 55 metres below the streets of Manhattan.

With 27,000 employees, the New York City subway is one of the largest urban rail networks in the world. About 4.5 million people are carried on the 600 trains every day.

The celebrations also focused on the efforts of men like William Barclay Parsons, the first chief engineer of the subway, and August Belmont, who paid for most of the original line. These men helped to plan, design and document (in photographs) the birth of the New York subway system.

LD -- FOLD

2. Answer these questions using the numbers in the box.

| 468 | 14 | 2 | 5 | 27,000 | 1,355 | 4 | ~~1904~~ | 10 | 277 | 4.5 million | 1,062 | 52 | 600 |

a) In which year was the underground first opened? _____1904_____

b) How much did it cost to ride on the subway in 1904? _____ cents

c) How much did the fare increase to after the first price rise? _____ cents

d) How long was the track when the subway system opened? _____ km

e) How many people work on the New York City subway? _____

f) How many people travel daily on the New York City subway? _____

g) How many trains are there on the subway system? _____

h) How much does it cost for a single fare today? _____ dollars

i) How much does it cost to buy an unlimited 24-hour ticket? _____ dollars

j) How many kilometres of track are there today? _____ km

k) Of them, how many kilometres are in use today? _____ km

l) How many subway stations are there on the network? _____

m) Of them, how many are underground? _____

n) How long is the longest stretch of line? _____ km

e-lesson

1. NYC subway centenary

On 26th October 1904, the New York City subway rumbled to life. It has been an eventful 100 years and in that time New York has risen to become one of the most influential cities of the twenty-first century. Read on to find out more.

Level

Pre-intermediate

How to use the lesson

1. You may want to find out from your students how many of them have been to New York and what their impressions were of the city.

2. Tell your students you are going to ask them to read a text and then answer some questions about the text. Give each student in the class a copy of the worksheet and ask them to fold along the line indicated and place on the table so that only the top half is showing. Then give them four minutes to read it and remember as many facts as they can.

3. When they have finished reading, ask your students to work together (in pairs or small groups) to answer the questions on the bottom half of the worksheet. Encourage them to try to answer as many as possible from memory.

4. Check answers in open class.

Answers
a) 1904
b) 5 cents
c) 10 cents
d) 14 km
e) 27,000
f) 4.5 million
g) 600
h) 2 dollars
i) 4 dollars
j) 1,355 km
k) 1,062 km
l) 468
m) 277
n) 52 km

2. Related Websites

Send your students to these websites, or just take a look yourself.

Some links to the New York City subway system:

http://www.mta.nyc.ny.us/nyct/cen/history.htm

http://www.mta.nyc.ny.us/nyct/subway/nyc100/

http://www.nyctimes.com/specials/nyc100/

Dragonslayer

1. Complete the story of St. George. Put **a**, **an**, **the** or – (nothing) into each space. The first one has been done as an example.

April 23rd is St. George's Day. St George is 1) __*the*__ patron saint of soldiers, archers, farmers and horse riders. He is also the patron saint of England.

St. George was born in Cappadocia (now in Eastern Turkey) in AD 270. He joined 2) _____ Roman army and became 3) _____ cavalry officer. He travelled all over 4) _____ Middle East and 5) _____ Europe with 6) _____ army.

When Emperor Diocletian learned that St. George was 7) _____ Christian (which was illegal), he had him arrested. St. George refused to deny his faith in Christ, even under extreme torture. He was eventually beheaded on April 23rd, AD 303, near Lydda in Palestine.

Stories of his courage soon spread across the Middle East and 8) _____ Europe. On one of 9) _____ walls in 10) _____ old Christian monastery in Egypt (St. Antony's), there is 11) _____ picture of St. George that dates back to 12) _____ 7th century.

2. Read the rest of the story. There are fourteen lines. Ten of them contain one extra word. The word is **the**, **an** or **a**. Find the extra words and write them in the column on the right. The first two lines have been done as examples.

1	King Richard I made St. George the patron saint of England. Richard's dream	___✓___
2	was to liberate Jerusalem. He organised an army (called the Crusaders) and left ~~the~~	__*the*__
3	England for the Holy Land in 1190 to fight the Muslim a leader Saladin. Richard's	_____
4	soldiers carried the emblem of St. George, a red cross on a white background, on their	_____
5	tunics and a shields.	_____
6	There are the many stories about St. George. One of the most famous legends is that	_____
7	he fought and killed a dragon in England. It is an unlikely that he ever visited England	_____
8	and even more unlikely that he killed a dragon. However, the dragon was a commonly	_____
9	used to represent the devil in the Middle Ages, which may be how the story started.	_____
10	More recently, on St. George's Day, 1564, one of an England's most famous writers	_____
11	was born: William Shakespeare. In a Shakespeare's play *Henry V*, the king finishes	_____
12	his the battle speech with the famous line "Cry 'God for Harry, England and St.	_____
13	George!'" This reference to St. George has helped to immortalise the saint in English	_____
14	tradition. Patriotic to the end, Shakespeare died on the St. George's Day in 1616.	_____

e-lesson

1. Dragonslayer

April 23rd is St. George's Day. He is famous in many countries in Europe and the Middle East. He is patron saint of England, although, unlike neighbours Ireland and Wales, the English don't have much in the way of a formal celebration to mark his feast day. A few pubs will probably hang the English flag (red cross on a white background) up outside. It may even surprise many English people to learn that not only was St. George not English, but probably never set foot in England during his life. Despite this, he is famous for having apparently slain a dragon on Dragon Hill at Uffington in Berkshire, England.

Level
Pre-intermediate and above

How to use the lesson
1. Give each of your students a copy of the worksheet and ask them to fold their piece of paper so that only the first exercise is visible.

2. Divide the class into pairs and ask the students to work together to complete the story of St. George by adding *a*, *an*, *the* or nothing.

3. Check answers in open class.

Answers
1. the   2. the   3. a   4. the   5. –   6. the   7. a   8. –   9. the   10. an   11. a   12. the

4. Tell your students they have four minutes to read the rest of the story (the bottom half of their piece of paper) and find the extra word *a*, *an*, or *the* (where appropriate) in each line. If they are not working very quickly, give them an extra minute.

5. When the time limit is up, stop your students and ask them to check their answers with the person sitting next to them.

6. Check answers in open class.

Answers
1. ✓   2. the   3. a   4. ✓   5. a   6. (1st) the   7. an   8. (2nd) a   9. ✓   10. an
11. a   12. (1st) the   13. ✓   14. the

2. Related Websites

Send your students to these websites, or just take a look yourself.
http://www.innotts.co.uk/asperges/george.html
A much more complete account of the life and legend of St. George
http://www.touregypt.net/featurestories/antony.htm
The beautiful St. Antony's Monastery
http://www.kidsturncentral.com/holidays/glossary/holidaysgloss.htm
Holidays around the world. Click on St. George's Day.
http://www.bbc.co.uk/london/yourlondon/stgeorges/your_views4.shtml
What the people say about St. George's Day. Why not write in yourself?

Rock Guitar Playing
Initial Stage

Compiled by
Tony Skinner and Merv Young
on behalf of
Registry Of Guitar Tutors
www.RGT.org

Printed and bound in Great Britain

A CIP record for this publication is available from the British Library
ISBN: 978-1-905908-29-5

Published by Registry Publications

Registry Mews, Wilton Rd, Bexhill, Sussex, TN40 1HY

Cover photo by Andreas Gradin/Fotolia. Design by JAK Images.
All musical compositions by Tony Skinner.

Compiled by

www.RGT.org

v.20110823

Contents

Introduction

This book is the first in a progressive series of ten handbooks designed for rock guitarists who wish to develop their playing and obtain a qualification. Although the primary intention of these handbooks is to prepare candidates for the Registry Of Guitar Tutors (RGT) rock guitar exams, the series provides a comprehensive structure that will help develop the abilities of any guitarist interested in rock music, whether or not intending to take an exam.

Those preparing for an exam should use this handbook in conjunction with the *Syllabus for Rock Guitar Playing* and the *Rock Guitar Exam Information Booklet* – both freely downloadable from the RGT website: **www.RGT.org**

Exam Outline

For the Initial Stage exam, candidates are required to perform TWO pieces of music. This book provides the notation for six specially-composed rock guitar pieces; the pieces are divided into two groups – Group A and Group B – and candidates should choose *one piece from each group* to perform in the exam. The pieces should be performed along to the backing tracks provided on the accompanying CD. The CD also includes a demonstration track of each piece for candidates to listen to and practise with prior to the exam.

A maximum of 50 marks may be achieved for the performance of each piece. To pass the exam candidates need a total of 65 marks. Candidates achieving 75 marks will be awarded a Merit certificate, or a Distinction certificate for 85 marks or above.

Exam Entry

An exam entry form is provided at the rear of this handbook. This is the only valid entry form for the RGT rock guitar playing exams.

Please note that if the entry form is detached and lost, it will not be replaced under any circumstances and the candidate will be required to obtain a replacement handbook to obtain another entry form.

The entry form includes a unique entry code to enable online entry via the RGT website **www.RGT.org**

Tuning

The CD provided with this handbook includes a tuning guide on Track 1 for candidates to use to practise tuning by ear.

For exam purposes guitars should be tuned to Standard Concert Pitch (A=440Hz). The use of an electronic tuner or other tuning aid is permitted. The examiner will not assist with tuning.

Notation

Within this handbook, three formats of notation are used: traditional notation, tablature and fretboxes – thereby ensuring that there is no doubt as to how to play the musical requirements. Each of these methods of notation is explained below.

Traditional Notation: Each line, and space between lines, represents a different note. Leger lines are used to extend the stave. For scales, string and fret numbers are printed below the notation: fret-hand fingering is shown with the numbers 1 2 3 4, with 0 indicating an open string; string numbers are shown in a circle.

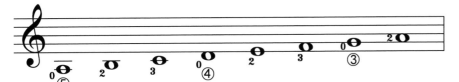

This example shows a one-octave A natural minor scale.

Tablature: Horizontal lines represent the strings (with the top line being the high E string). The numbers on the string lines refer to the frets. 0 on a line means play that string open (unfretted).

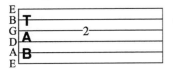

This example means play at the second fret on the third string.

Fretboxes: Vertical lines represent the strings – with the line furthest to the right representing the high E string. Horizontal lines represent the frets. The numbers on the lines show the recommended fingering. 1 represents the index finger, 2 = the long middle finger, 3 = the ring finger, 4 = the little finger. The example below means play with the second finger at the second fret on the G string.

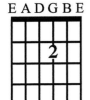

If a 0 appears above a string line, this indicates that the open string should be played.

If, in a chord fretbox, an X appears above a string line, this indicates that this string should not be played.

Fingering Options

The fret-hand fingerings that have been provided for chords and scales are those that are most likely to be effective for the widest range of players at this level. However, there are a variety of alternative fingerings that could be used, and any systematic and effective fingerings that produce a good musical result will be acceptable; there is no requirement to use the exact fingerings shown within this handbook. In addition, it should be noted that the optimal fingering for playing a scale might not always be the most effective fingering for playing a performance piece that is based on that scale; when playing the performance pieces some notes might be more easily fretted with a fingering other than that which would be most effective if just playing the scale.

Chords and Scales

Candidates will need to be fully familiar with the chords and scales listed below in order to be properly prepared for performing the set pieces in the exam, as the pieces have been specially composed to incorporate these chords and scales.

Chords

Here is the range of chords that are included in the exam pieces.

• Minor chords:	Am Em
• Fifth (power) chords:	A5 E5
• Major chords:	G D

Am – A minor

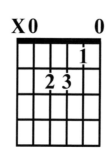

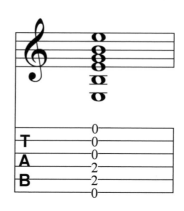

Em – E minor

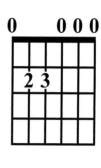

A5 – A fifth (power chord)

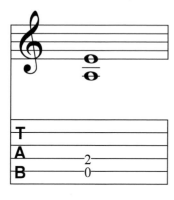

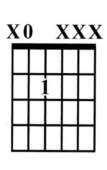

E5 – E fifth (power chord)

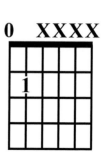

6

G – G major*

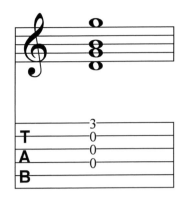 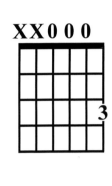

D – D major

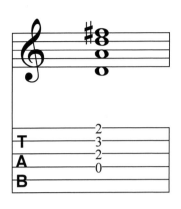 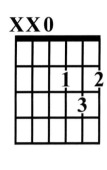

 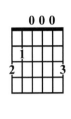

*To enable young players, especially those with small hands, to cope with the physical challenge of playing a G major chord, the simplified four-string version of the chord as shown above (technically named G/D) is utilised within the pieces set for this exam level. For reference only, notation showing the standard full version of the open position G major chord is also provided.

Scales

Here are the scales that are utilised in the exam performance pieces.

A natural minor scale – 1 octave
A B C D E F G A

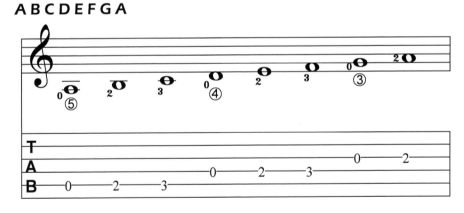 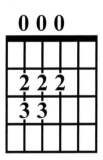

E pentatonic minor scale – 1 octave
E G A B D E

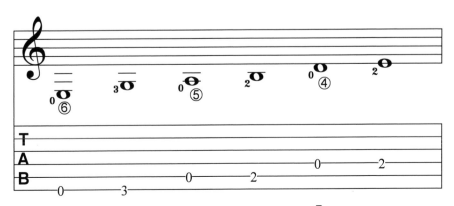 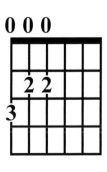

Prepared Performances

Candidates should choose and perform TWO of the pieces from this chapter – one from Group A and one from Group B.

The melody lines and riffs in the Group A pieces are all based on the A natural minor scale, whereas those in the Group B pieces are based on the E pentatonic minor scale. All pieces also incorporate some of the chords listed in the previous chapter. Therefore, regular practice of all the scales and chords listed for the grade will undoubtedly aid the learning and performance of the pieces, and so it is highly recommended that candidates acquire a thorough working knowledge of the appropriate scales and chords prior to attempting to play the pieces.

The CD that accompanies this book includes a backing track for each piece for the candidate to practise playing along to. There is no need to bring the CD to the exam, as the examiner will provide the necessary backing tracks during the exam.
The CD also features each track being performed in full for demonstration purposes and as an aid to learning.

Exam format

Candidates' performances should be accurate reproductions of the pieces as notated in this book. Alternative fingerings and playing positions can be adopted if preferred, provided the overall musical result is not altered from the recorded version.

Performances do not need to be from memory; candidates should remember to bring their handbook to the exam should they wish to refer to the notation.

Prior to the performances commencing, candidates will be allowed a brief 'soundcheck' so that they can choose their sound and volume level. Candidates do not need to emulate the guitar sound used on the demonstration recording; candidates can use either a clean or a distorted guitar sound for their performance of the pieces, and can bring their own distortion or other effects units to the exam *providing that* they can set them up promptly and unaided.

In order to achieve a high mark in the exam, performances should be fully accurate and confidently presented. Timing, clarity and technical control should be secure throughout.

Quiet As A Bulldog [Group A]

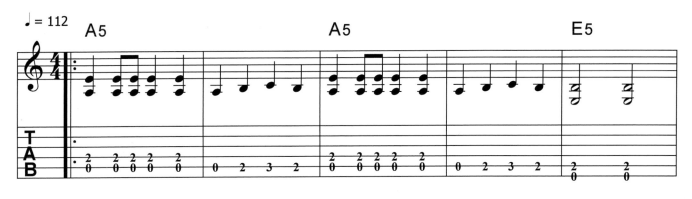

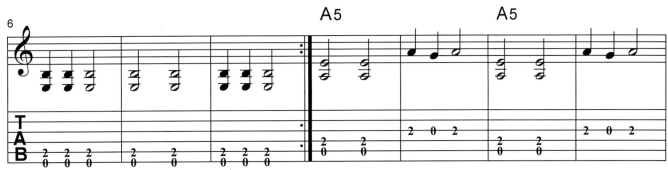

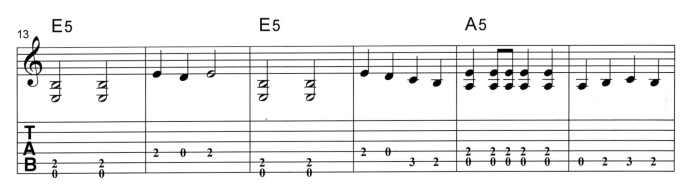

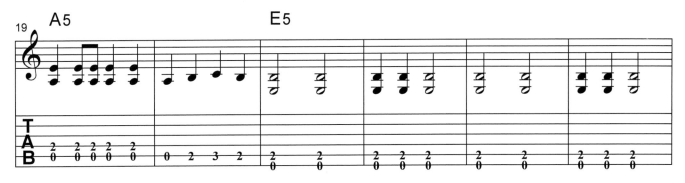

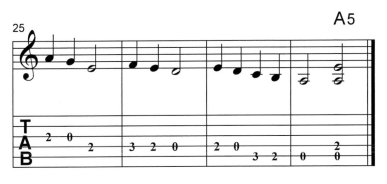

LISTEN AND LEARN

This piece can be heard on CD track 2

A backing track is provided on CD track 3

Firecracker [Group A]

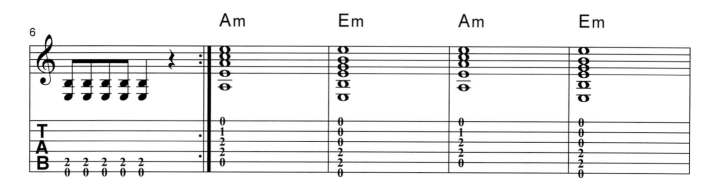

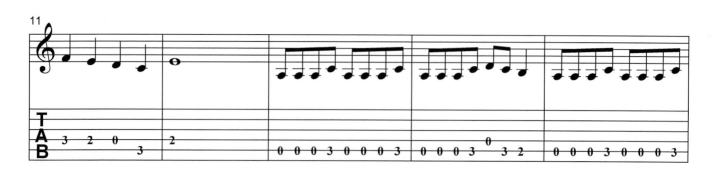

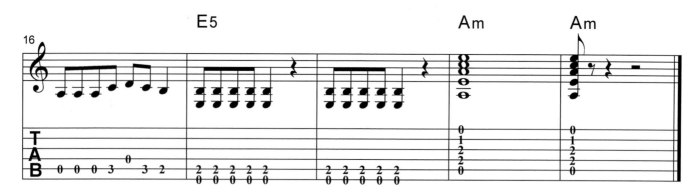

LISTEN AND LEARN

This piece can be heard on CD track 4
A backing track is provided on CD track 5

The Jaguar [Group A]

♩ = 100

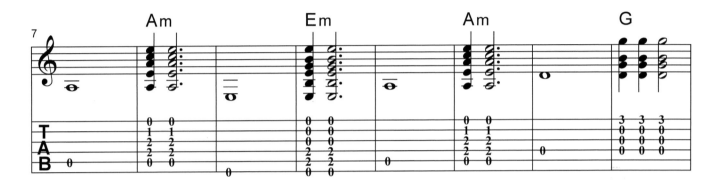

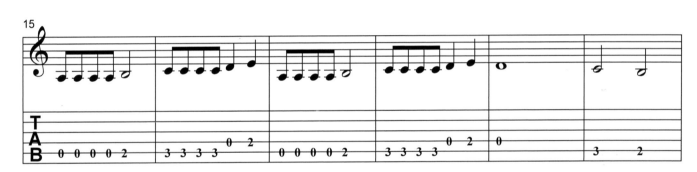

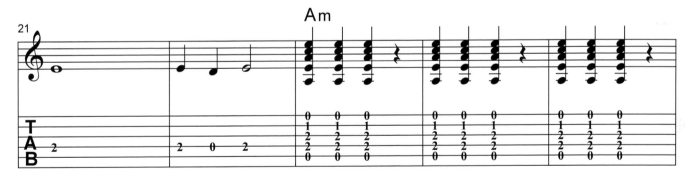

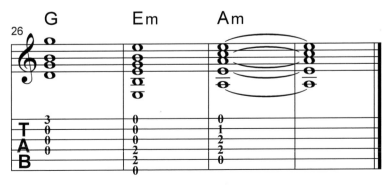

LISTEN AND LEARN

This piece can be heard on CD track 6

A backing track is provided on CD track 7

Jump The Barrier [Group B]

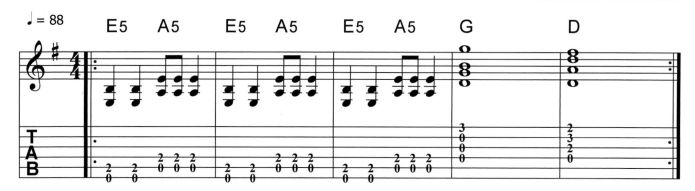

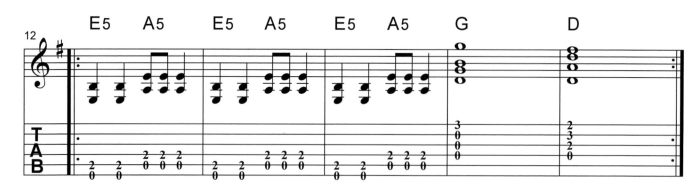

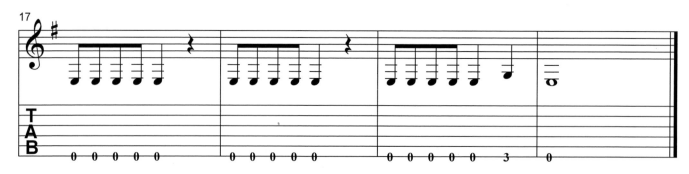

LISTEN AND LEARN

This piece can be heard on CD track 8
A backing track is provided on CD track 9

Armour Plated [Group B]

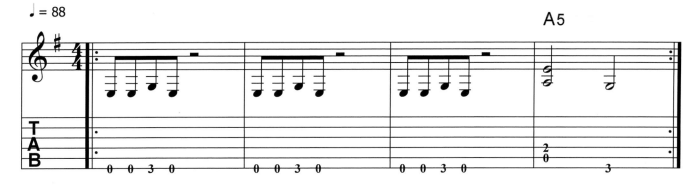

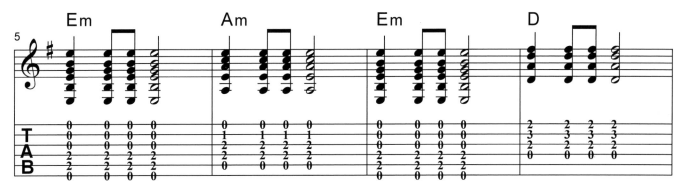

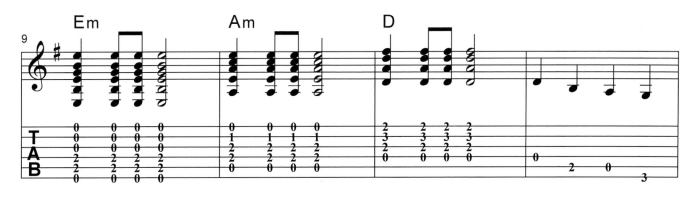

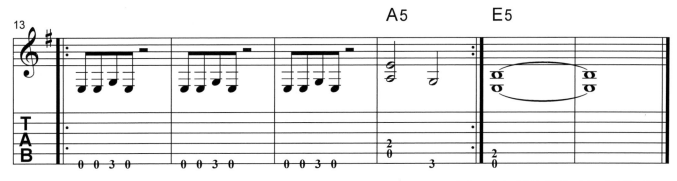

LISTEN AND LEARN

This piece can be heard on CD track 10
A backing track is provided on CD track 11

Missing In Action [Group B]

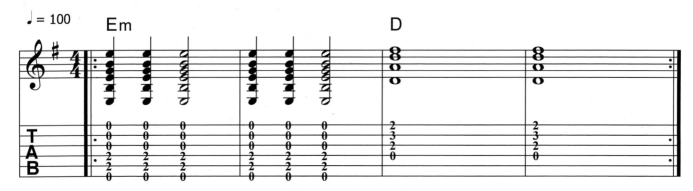

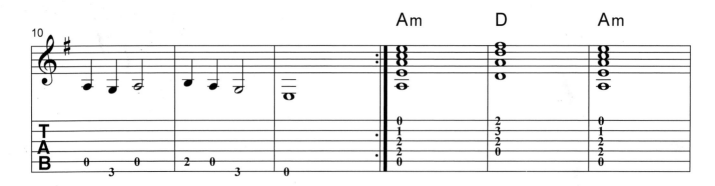

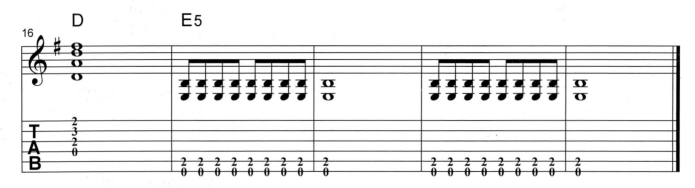

LISTEN AND LEARN

This piece can be heard on CD track 12
A backing track is provided on CD track 13